This journal belongs to:

_____

If found, please contact:

_____

Make it Happen

Amor fati

GOLF DATA

JOURNAL

PERFORMANCE STATISTICS ABOUT YOUR GAME

MAKINGACLUBCHAMPION.COM

Also by MakingAClubChampion.com

Short Game: 125 Yards and In
Long Game: 290 Yards and In

"Do what you fear and fear disappears."

David Joseph Schwartz. The Magic of Thinking Big

WHY YOU NEED THIS BOOK
(And the others)

*"If you are going to practice you need to practice against numbers.
Otherwise, you do not know if you are getting any better."*

- Dave Alred, Pressure Principle

"Discipline equals freedom."
- Jocko Willink, Extreme Ownership

Whether you have selected Golf Data, Long Game or Short Game. They all try and do one thing. <u>Getting you to record how you spend your time practicing.</u>

Keep them in your golf bag and travel with them wherever you play.

Here is a breakdown on what each book will offer you.

Golf Data - Performance Statistics About Your Game

You will learn:

- How to keep a record of all your tournament and practice rounds.
- How to analyse how many fairways, greens, putts you take during your round.
- How to track what side of the course you keep hitting your drives.
- How to identify your common misses with all approach shots.

Long Game - 290 yards and In, Driving Range Journal

You will learn:

- How to make your range time more effective.
- How to implement pressure and real-life tournament conditions.
- How to increase your focus through accountability.
- How to eliminate one side of the course.

Short Game - 125 yards and In

You will learn:

- How to master your wedge game through yardages systems like Luke Donald.
- How to identify your common misses with all your approach shots within 125 yards.
- How to "gamify" your short game sessions against the worlds best.
- How to implement go to shots you can rely on in tournament conditions.

Each book will give you the creativity to explore your own unique way of playing the game. It doesn't take much to become impressive when you have a solid structure behind the time invested.

Although the dream is to play your best carefree golf. Remember: *"Everyone wants to be famous, nobody wants to do the work."* Kevin Hart.

It is time to let go of your ego and detach yourself from the end goal of any particular day. The only thing that matters is that you showed up.

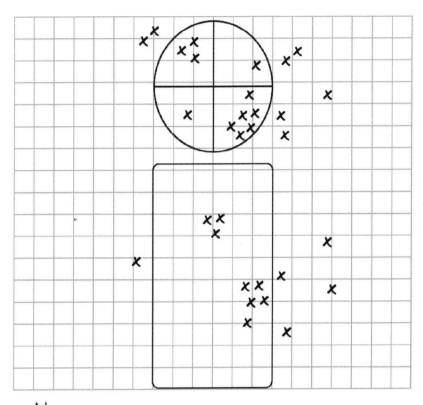

Notes

- Practice drawing the ball next session.

- Work on distance control 125 yards and in.

- Practice bunker shots. 50 push-ups if you do
  not make more than 6/10.

- Putting - work on alignment and path.

Course: _____   Date: *Sep 12, 2017*

EXAMPLE PAGE

FAIRWAYS	8/13 - 62%	LEFT 9	RIGHT 4
GREENS	11/18 - 61%	LEFT 12	RIGHT 6
UP & DOWNS	4/8 - 50%		
PUTTS	29		
Sand saves	1/5 - 20%		
125 Yards & In	2/11 - 18%		
Putts inside 15 ft	2/6 - 33%		
3 putts	0		
18 HOLE SCORE	76		

To calculate %- Divide your total hit by the total for the course & multiply by100:
e.g. Fairways hit = 8 ÷ 13 (course total) = 0.62 x 100 = 62%

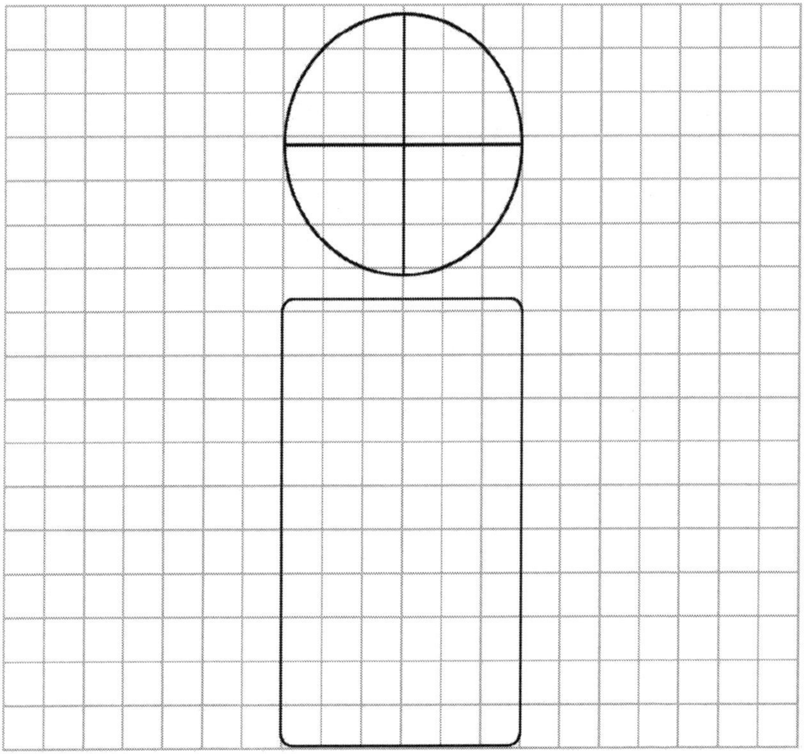

Notes

_____

_____

_____

_____

_____

_____

_____

Course: Date:

"If you set your goals ridiculously high and it's a failure, you will fail above everyone else's success."

– James Cameron

FAIRWAYS		LEFT	RIGHT
GREENS		LEFT	RIGHT
UP & DOWNS			
PUTTS			
18 HOLE SCORE			

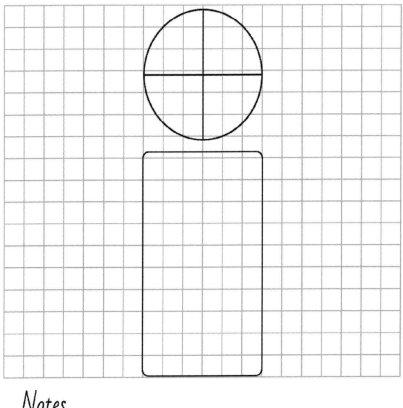

Notes

_____

_____

_____

_____

_____

_____

_____

_____

Course: _____ **Date:** _____

"We are what we repeatedly do. Excellence, therefore, is not an act but a habit."

– Aristotle

FAIRWAYS		LEFT	RIGHT
GREENS		LEFT	RIGHT
UP & DOWNS			
PUTTS			
18 HOLE SCORE			

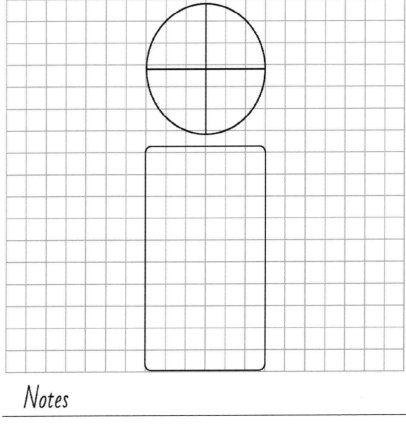

Notes

_____

_____

_____

_____

_____

_____

_____

Course: _____   Date: _____

"The best way out is always through."

— Robert Frost

FAIRWAYS		LEFT	RIGHT
GREENS		LEFT	RIGHT
UP & DOWNS			
PUTTS			
18 HOLE SCORE			

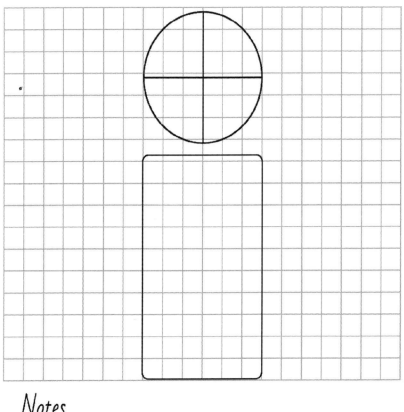

Notes

Course: _____ **Date:** _____

"I know for sure that what we dwell on is who we become."

– Oprah Winfrey •

FAIRWAYS		LEFT	RIGHT
GREENS		LEFT	RIGHT
UP & DOWNS			
PUTTS			
18 HOLE SCORE			

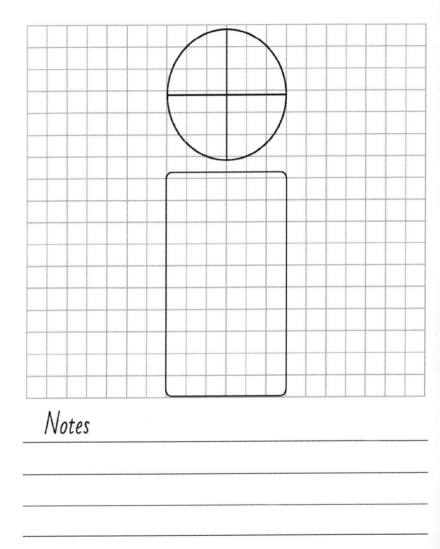

Notes

Course: Date:

"You must be the change you want to see in the world."

– Mahatma Gandhi

		LEFT	RIGHT
FAIRWAYS		LEFT	RIGHT
GREENS		LEFT	RIGHT
UP & DOWNS			
PUTTS			
18 HOLE SCORE			

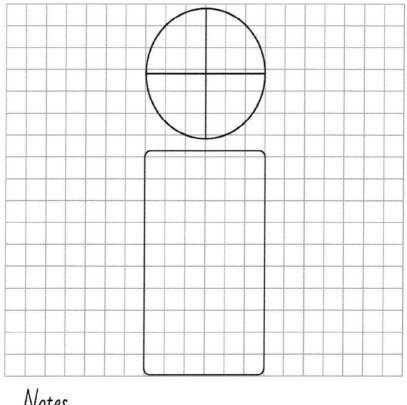

Notes

Course: _____ **Date:** _____

"What you get by achieving your goals is not as important as what you become by achieving your goals."

— Goethe

		LEFT	RIGHT
FAIRWAYS			
GREENS		LEFT	RIGHT
UP & DOWNS			
PUTTS			
18 HOLE SCORE			

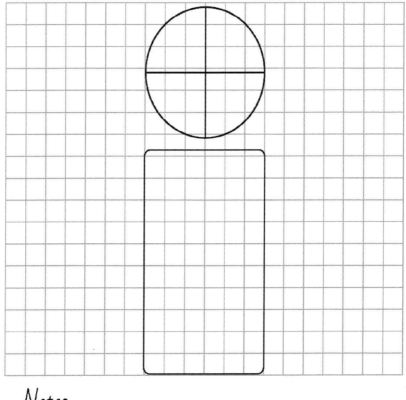

Notes

_____

_____

_____

_____

_____

_____

_____

Course: _____ **Date:** _____

"You can get everything in life you want if you will just help enough other people get what they want."

– Zig Ziglar

		LEFT	RIGHT
FAIRWAYS		LEFT	RIGHT
GREENS		LEFT	RIGHT
UP & DOWNS			
PUTTS			
18 HOLE SCORE			

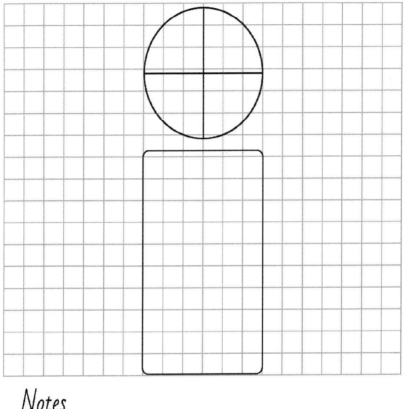

Notes

Course: Date:

"Whatever you do will be insignificant, but it is very important that you do it."

– Mahatma Gandhi

		LEFT	RIGHT
FAIRWAYS			
GREENS		LEFT	RIGHT
UP & DOWNS			
PUTTS			
18 HOLE SCORE			

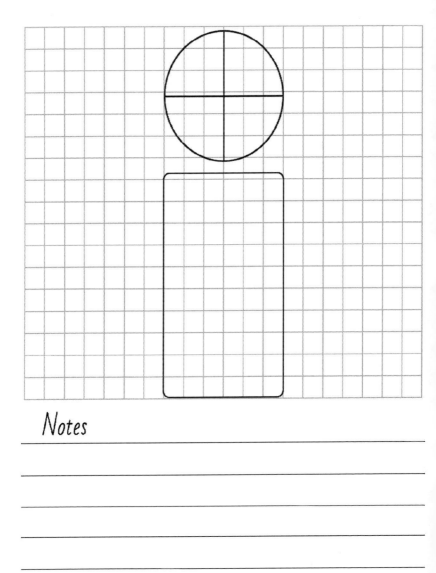

Notes

Course: Date:

"Desire is the starting point of all achievement, not a hope, not a wish, but a keen pulsating desire which transcends everything."
– Napoleon Hill

		LEFT	RIGHT
FAIRWAYS		LEFT	RIGHT
GREENS		LEFT	RIGHT
UP & DOWNS			
PUTTS			
18 HOLE SCORE			

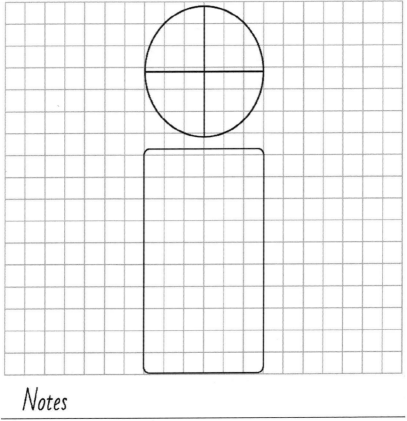

Notes

Course: _____ Date: _____

"Failure is the condiment that gives success its flavor."

– Truman Capote

		LEFT	RIGHT
FAIRWAYS		LEFT	RIGHT
GREENS		LEFT	RIGHT
UP & DOWNS			
PUTTS			
18 HOLE SCORE			

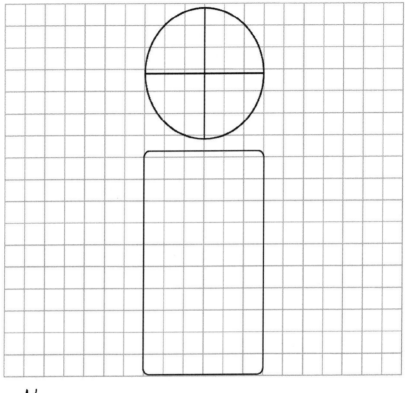

Notes

_____

_____

_____

_____

_____

_____

_____

Course: _____   Date: _____

"Vision without action is daydream. Action without vision is nightmare."

— Japanese Proverb

		LEFT	RIGHT
FAIRWAYS		LEFT	RIGHT
GREENS			
UP & DOWNS			
PUTTS			
18 HOLE SCORE			

Well done you! Get back to work!

PLAYER PERFORMANCE STATS

JUSTIN THOMAS	SKILL	%	RANK
	Fairways	55	162nd
	GIR (%)	67	46th
HEIGHT 5 ft, 10 in WEIGHT 145 lbs	Up & Downs	60.39	54th
	Puts Per Round	28.25	5th
	Driving Distance	309.7	8th
BIRTHPLACE Louisville, Kentucky	Sand Saves	48.21	122nd
COLLEGE University of Alabama	Birdie Average	4.48	2nd
TURNED PRO 2013	Scoring Average	69.39	2nd

JORDAN SPEITH	SKILL	%	RANK
	Fairways	60	101st
	GIR (%)	70.01	4th
HEIGHT 6 ft, 1 in WEIGHT 185 lbs	Up & Downs	61.76	34th
	Puts Per Round	28.45	20th
	Driving Distance	295.6	75th
BIRTHPLACE Dallas, Texas	Sand Saves	55.79	33rd
COLLEGE University of Texas	Birdie Average	4.49	1st
TURNED PRO 2012	Scoring Average	68.84	1st

How do your stats compare to the world's best?

PLAYER PERFORMANCE STATS

DUSTIN JOHNSON	SKILL	%	RANK
	Fairways	56.97	143rd
	GIR (%)	69.52	9th
HEIGHT 6 ft, 4 in	Up & Downs	62.76	23rd
WEIGHT 190 lbs	Puts Per Round	29.1	99th
BIRTHPLACE Columbia, South Carolina	Driving Distance	315	2nd
COLLEGE Coastal Carolina University	Sand Saves	44.32	165th
TURNED PRO 2007	Birdie Average	3.99	11th
	Scoring Average	69.549	7th

HIDEKI MATSUYAMA	SKILL	%	RANK
	Fairways	58.61	121st
	GIR (%)	69.01	16th
HEIGHT 5 ft, 11 in	Up & Downs	61.56	37th
WEIGHT 198 lbs	Puts Per Round	28.86	62nd
BIRTHPLACE Ehime, Japan	Driving Distance	303.3	26th
COLLEGE Tohoku Fukushi University	Sand Saves	50.88	96th
TURNED PRO 2013	Birdie Average	4.29	3rd
	Scoring Average	69.62	10th

Which stat do you need to work on the most? Identify it and get to work.

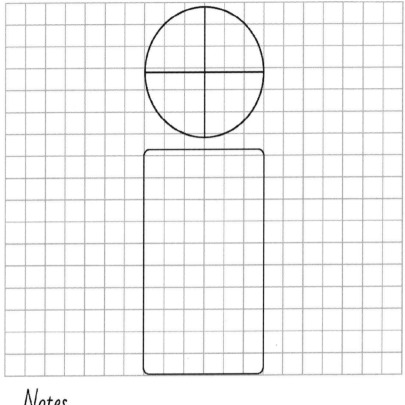

Notes

Course: _____   Date: _____

"In any situation, the best thing you can do is the right thing; the next best thing you can do is the wrong thing; the worst thing you can do is nothing."

— Theodore Roosevelt

		LEFT	RIGHT
FAIRWAYS			
GREENS		LEFT	RIGHT
UP & DOWNS			
PUTTS			
18 HOLE SCORE			

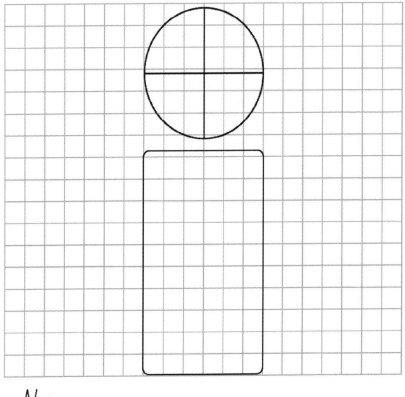

Notes

Course: _____ Date: _____

"If you keep saying things are going to be bad, you have a chance of being a prophet."

— Isaac B. Singer

		LEFT	RIGHT
FAIRWAYS			
GREENS		LEFT	RIGHT
UP & DOWNS			
PUTTS			
18 HOLE SCORE			

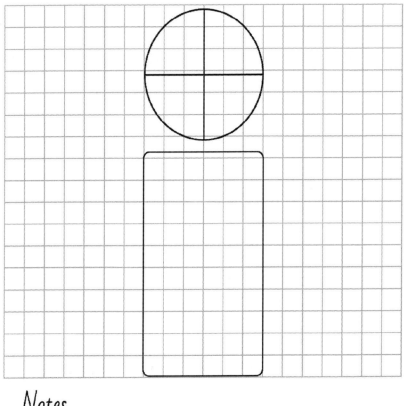

Notes

Course: _____ **Date:** _____

"Success consists of doing the common things of life uncommonly well."

– Unknown

		LEFT	RIGHT
FAIRWAYS			
GREENS		LEFT	RIGHT
UP & DOWNS			
PUTTS			
18 HOLE SCORE			

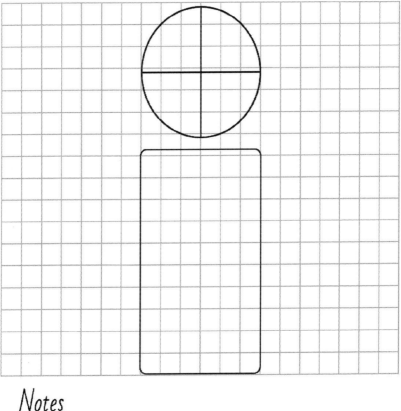

Notes

Course: _____ **Date:** _____

"Losers visualize the penalties of failure. Winners visualize the rewards of success."

– Unknown

		LEFT	RIGHT
FAIRWAYS		LEFT	RIGHT
GREENS			
UP & DOWNS			
PUTTS			
18 HOLE SCORE			

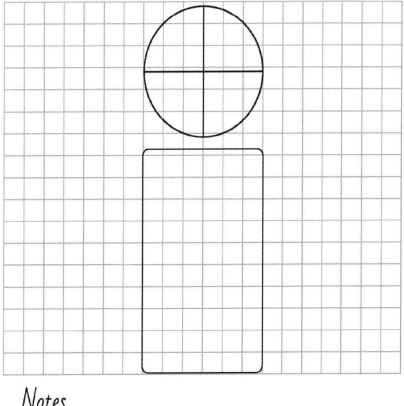

Notes

Course: _____ **Date:** _____

"Some succeed because they are destined. Some succeed because they are determined."

– Unknown

		LEFT	RIGHT
FAIRWAYS		LEFT	RIGHT
GREENS		LEFT	RIGHT
UP & DOWNS			
PUTTS			
18 HOLE SCORE			

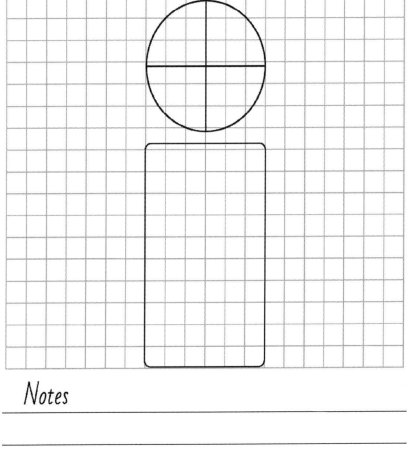

Notes

Course: _____   Date: _____

"Experience is what you get when you don't get what you want."

– Dan Stanford

		LEFT	RIGHT
FAIRWAYS		LEFT	RIGHT
GREENS		LEFT	RIGHT
UP & DOWNS			
PUTTS			
18 HOLE SCORE			

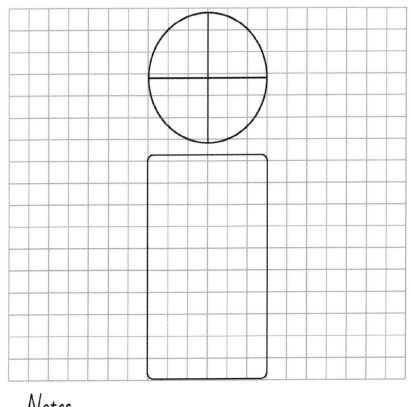

Notes

_____

_____

_____

_____

_____

_____

_____

_____

Course: _____ **Date:** _____

"Setting an example is not the main means of influencing others; it is the only means."

– Albert Einstein

		LEFT	RIGHT
FAIRWAYS		LEFT	RIGHT
GREENS		LEFT	RIGHT
UP & DOWNS			
PUTTS			
18 HOLE SCORE			

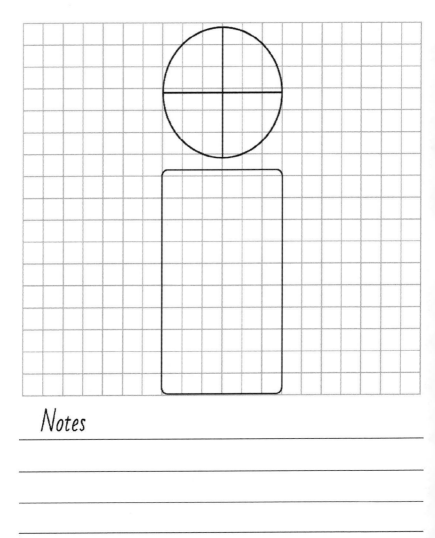

Notes

Course: _____   Date: _____

"A happy person is not a person in a certain set of circumstances, but rather a person with a certain set of attitudes."

— Hugh Downs

		LEFT	RIGHT
FAIRWAYS			
GREENS		LEFT	RIGHT
UP & DOWNS			
PUTTS			
18 HOLE SCORE			

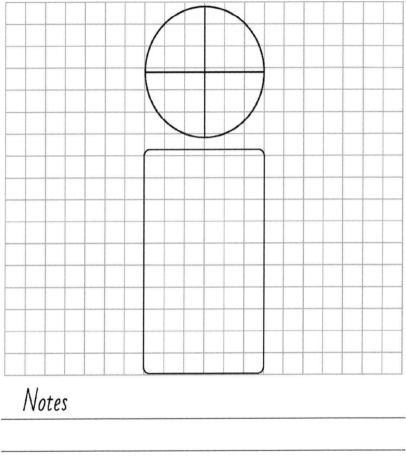

Notes
_____
_____
_____
_____
_____
_____
_____

Course: _____ Date: _____

"If you want to test your memory, try to recall what you were worrying about one year ago today."

– E. Joseph Cossman

		LEFT	RIGHT
FAIRWAYS		LEFT	RIGHT
GREENS		LEFT	RIGHT
UP & DOWNS			
PUTTS			
18 HOLE SCORE			

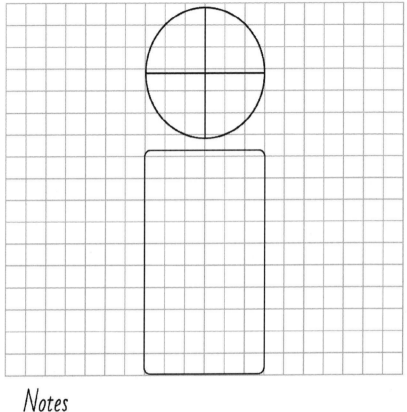

Notes

Course: _____ **Date:** _____

"Whenever you find yourself on the side of the majority, it's time to pause and reflect."

— Mark Twain

		LEFT	RIGHT
FAIRWAYS			
GREENS		LEFT	RIGHT
UP & DOWNS			
PUTTS			
18 HOLE SCORE			

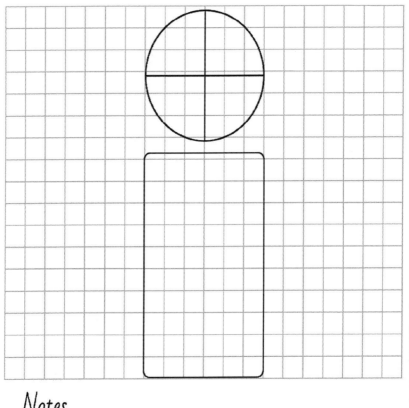

Notes

_____

_____

_____

_____

_____

_____

_____

_____

Course: _____ **Date:** _____

"The surest way not to fail is to determine to succeed."

– Richard B. Sheridan

FAIRWAYS		LEFT	RIGHT
GREENS		LEFT	RIGHT
UP & DOWNS			
PUTTS			
18 HOLE SCORE			

PLAYER PERFORMANCE STATS

JOHN RAHM	SKILL	%	RANK
	Fairways	58.66	120th
	GIR (%)	68.61	21st
HEIGHT	Up & Downs	63.33	13th
6 ft, 2 in	Puts Per Round	28.88	66th
WEIGHT 220 lbs	Driving Distance	305.8	20th
BIRTHPLACE Barrika, Spain	Sand Saves	59.12	12th
COLLEGE Arizona State University	Birdie Average	4.11	7th
TURNED PRO 2016	Scoring Average	69.56	8th

RICKIE FOWLER	SKILL	%	RANK
	Fairways	300.3	41st
	GIR (%)	63.91	52nd
HEIGHT	Up & Downs	63.86	8th
5 ft, 9 in	Puts Per Round	28.3	9th
WEIGHT 150 lbs	Driving Distance	300.3	41st
BIRTHPLACE Murrieta, California	Sand Saves	68.66	1st
COLLEGE Oklahoma State University	Birdie Average	4.28	4th
TURNED PRO 2009	Scoring Average	69.08	2nd

What is your GIR percentage?

PLAYER PERFORMANCE STATS

JUSTIN ROSE	SKILL	%	RANK
	Fairways	58.32	125th
	GIR (%)	68.06	25th
HEIGHT 6 ft, 3 in	Up & Downs	58.97	92nd
WEIGHT 195 lbs	Puts Per Round	29.16	112th
	Driving Distance	300.9	35th
BIRTHPLACE Johannesburg, South Africa	Sand Saves	55.93	31st
COLLEGE	Birdie Average	4.09	8th
TURNED PRO 1998	Scoring Average	69.699	11th

PAUL CASEY	SKILL	%	RANK
	Fairways	64.13	49th
	GIR (%)	70.06	3rd
HEIGHT 5 ft, 10 in	Up & Downs	64.12	7th
WEIGHT 180 lbs	Puts Per Round	29.03	86th
BIRTHPLACE Cheltenham, England	Driving Distance	297.5	58th
	Sand Saves	39.17	184th
COLLEGE Arizona State University	Birdie Average	3.87	19th
TURNED PRO 2000	Scoring Average	69.469	5th

How well do you know your yardages?

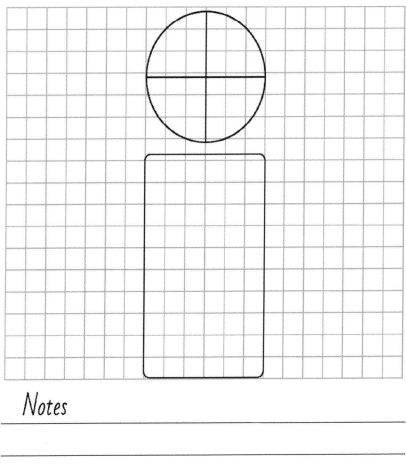

Notes

Course: _____ Date: _____

"Act or accept."

— Anonymous

		LEFT	RIGHT
FAIRWAYS			
GREENS		LEFT	RIGHT
UP & DOWNS			
PUTTS			
18 HOLE SCORE			

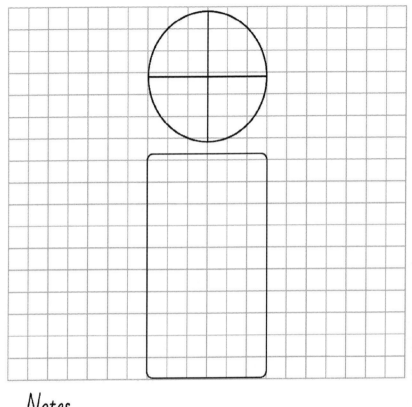

Notes

Course: _____ **Date:** _____

"Fall down seven times, get up eight."

– Japanese Proverb

		LEFT	RIGHT
FAIRWAYS		LEFT	RIGHT
GREENS		LEFT	RIGHT
UP & DOWNS			
PUTTS			
18 HOLE SCORE			

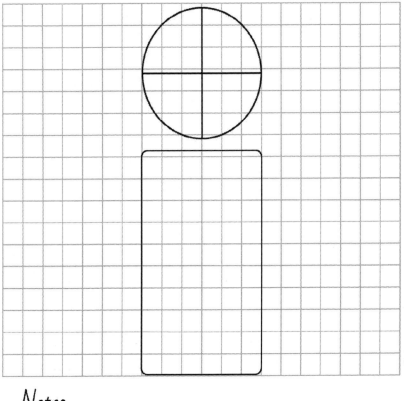

Notes

_____

_____

_____

_____

_____

_____

_____

How's the game looking?

Course: _____   **Date:** _____

"The difference between ordinary and extraordinary is that little extra."

– Unknown

		LEFT	RIGHT
FAIRWAYS		LEFT	RIGHT
GREENS		LEFT	RIGHT
UP & DOWNS			
PUTTS			
18 HOLE SCORE			

Noticing any common themes with your mistakes? Identify them and get back to work.

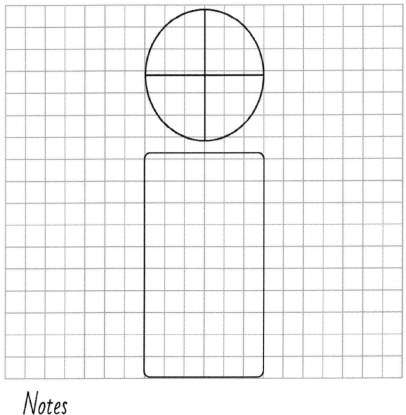

Notes

Course: _____ **Date:** _____

"The best way to predict the future is to create it."

– Unknown

FAIRWAYS		LEFT	RIGHT
GREENS		LEFT	RIGHT
UP & DOWNS			
PUTTS			
18 HOLE SCORE			

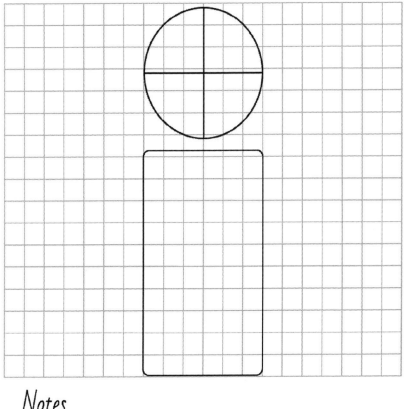

Notes

Course: _____   Date: _____

"Success is the ability to go from failure to failure without losing your enthusiasm."

– Sir Winston Churchill

		LEFT	RIGHT
FAIRWAYS		LEFT	RIGHT
GREENS		LEFT	RIGHT
UP & DOWNS			
PUTTS			
18 HOLE SCORE			

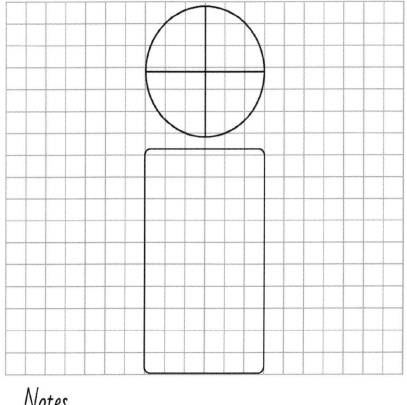

Notes

_____

_____

_____

_____

_____

_____

_____

Course: _____ **Date:** _____

"Attitudes are contagious. Make yours worth catching."

– Unknown

		LEFT	RIGHT
FAIRWAYS			
GREENS		LEFT	RIGHT
UP & DOWNS			
PUTTS			
18 HOLE SCORE			

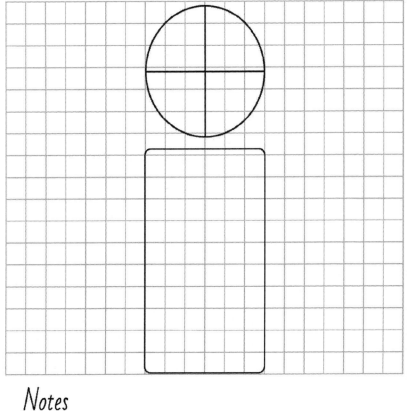

Notes

Course: _____ Date: _____

"There are only two rules for being successful. One, figure out exactly what you want to do, and two, do it."

— Mario Cuomo

		LEFT	RIGHT
FAIRWAYS			
GREENS		LEFT	RIGHT
UP & DOWNS			
PUTTS			
18 HOLE SCORE			

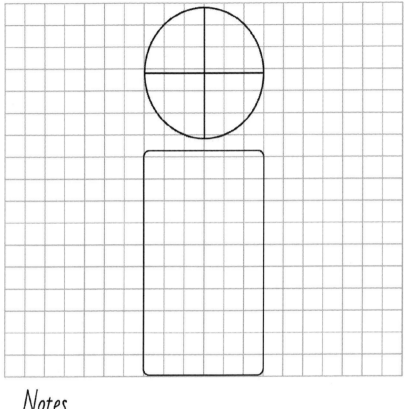

Notes

Course: _____   Date: _____

"Success is a state of mind. If you want success, start thinking of yourself as a success."

– Dr. Joyce Brothers

		LEFT	RIGHT
FAIRWAYS		LEFT	RIGHT
GREENS		LEFT	RIGHT
UP & DOWNS			
PUTTS			
18 HOLE SCORE			

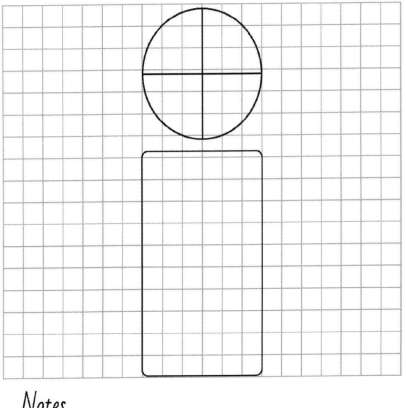

Notes

_____

_____

_____

_____

_____

_____

_____

Course: _____   Date: _____

"Ever tried. Ever failed. No matter. Try Again. Fail again. Fail better."

– Samuel Beckett

		LEFT	RIGHT
FAIRWAYS		LEFT	RIGHT
GREENS		LEFT	RIGHT
UP & DOWNS			
PUTTS			
18 HOLE SCORE			

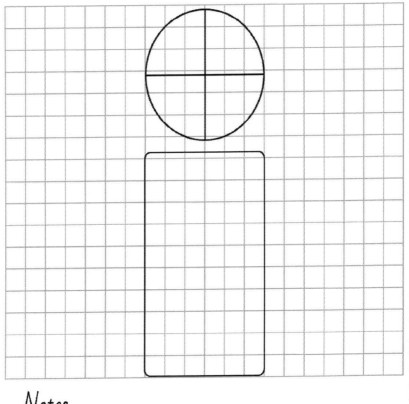

Notes

Course: _____ **Date:** _____

"An obstacle is often a stepping stone."

– Prescott

FAIRWAYS		LEFT	RIGHT
GREENS		LEFT	RIGHT
UP & DOWNS			
PUTTS			
18 HOLE SCORE			

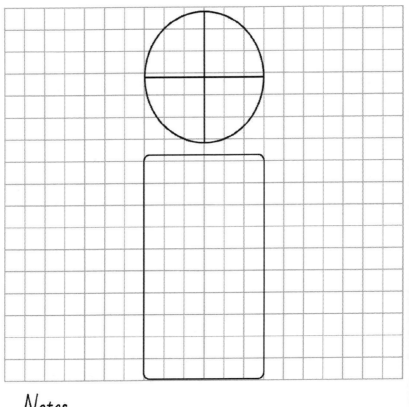

Notes

_____

_____

_____

_____

_____

_____

_____

Course: _____   **Date:** _____

"Life is 10% what happens to us and 90% how we react to it."

– Denis P. Kimbro

		LEFT	RIGHT
FAIRWAYS		LEFT	RIGHT
GREENS		LEFT	RIGHT
UP & DOWNS			
PUTTS			
18 HOLE SCORE			

PLAYER PERFORMANCE STATS

SERGIO GARCIA	SKILL	%	RANK
	Fairways	62.33	75th
	GIR (%)	69.62	8th
HEIGHT 5 ft, 10 in	Up & Downs	61.65	35th
WEIGHT 180 lbs	Puts Per Round	29.37	142nd
BIRTHPLACE Castellon, Spain	Driving Distance	301.9	30th
COLLEGE	Sand Saves	53.1	64th
TURNED PRO 1999	Birdie Average	3.66	67th
	Scoring Average	69.596	9th

RORY McILroy	SKILL	%	RANK
	Fairways	55.06	161st
	GIR (%)	65.63	96th
HEIGHT 5 ft, 10 in	Up & Downs	62.29	28th
WEIGHT 160 lbs	Puts Per Round	28.75	51st
BIRTHPLACE Holywood, Northern Ireland	Driving Distance	317.2	1st
COLLEGE	Sand Saves	63.24	3rd
TURNED PRO 2007	Birdie Average	3.85	24th
	Scoring Average	69.529	6th

What are your Up & Down percentages like?

PLAYER PERFORMANCE STATS

PHIL MICKELSON	SKILL	%	RANK
	Fairways	55.05	162nd
	GIR (%)	62.85	163rd
HEIGHT 6 ft, 3 in	Up & Downs	60	67th
WEIGHT 200 lbs	Puts Per Round	28.25	5th
BIRTHPLACE San Diego, California	Driving Distance	293.5	89th
COLLEGE Arizona State University	Sand Saves	53.33	58th
TURNED PRO 1992	Birdie Average	3.86	20th
	Scoring Average	70.16	28th

IAN POULTER	SKILL	%	RANK
	Fairways	62.55	74th
	GIR (%)	64.46	126th
HEIGHT 6 ft, 1 in	Up & Downs	67.36	1st
WEIGHT 189 lbs	Puts Per Round	28.44	18th
BIRTHPLACE Stevenage, England	Driving Distance	283.5	159th
COLLEGE Barclay School	Sand Saves	59.29	11th
TURNED PRO 1995	Birdie Average	3.46	117th
	Scoring Average	70.04	22nd

How much time do you dedicate to chipping around the green?

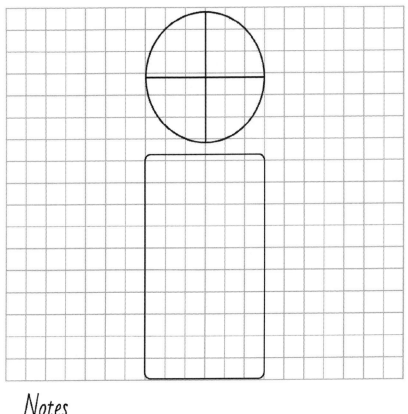

Notes

_____

_____

_____

_____

_____

_____

_____

Course: _____   **Date:** _____

"You are what you think about all day long."

– Dr. Robert Schuller

		LEFT	RIGHT
FAIRWAYS		LEFT	RIGHT
GREENS		LEFT	RIGHT
UP & DOWNS			
PUTTS			
18 HOLE SCORE			

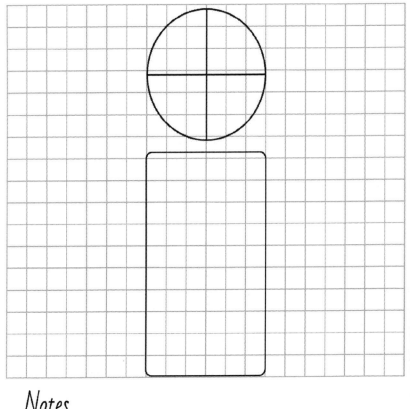

Notes

_____
_____
_____
_____
_____
_____
_____
_____

Course: _____   Date: _____

*"Success is not to be measured by the position someone has reached in life,
but the obstacles he has overcome while trying to succeed."*

— Brooker T. Washington

FAIRWAYS		LEFT	RIGHT
GREENS		LEFT	RIGHT
UP & DOWNS			
PUTTS			
18 HOLE SCORE			

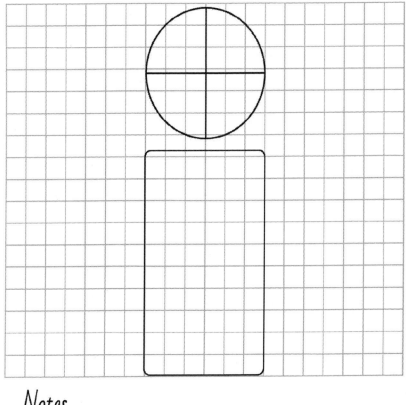

Notes

Course: _____   Date: _____

"I would rather die of passion than of boredom."

– Vincent van Gogh

		LEFT	RIGHT
FAIRWAYS		LEFT	RIGHT
GREENS		LEFT	RIGHT
UP & DOWNS			
PUTTS			
18 HOLE SCORE			

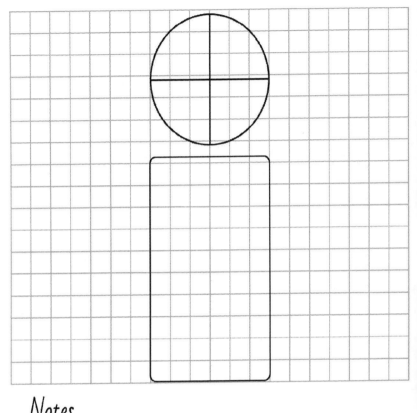

Notes

Course: _____   Date: _____

"I have been impressed with the urgency of doing. Knowing is not enough; we must apply. Being willing is not enough; we must do."

– Leonardo da Vinci

		LEFT	RIGHT
FAIRWAYS		LEFT	RIGHT
GREENS		LEFT	RIGHT
UP & DOWNS			
PUTTS			
18 HOLE SCORE			

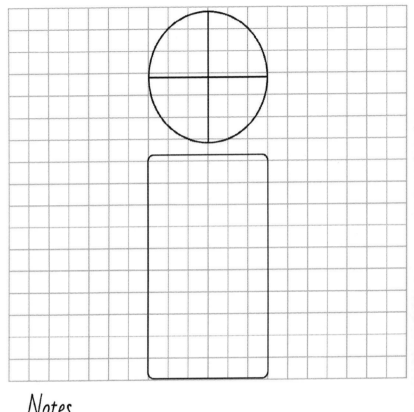

Notes

Course: _____ **Date:** _____

"Certain things catch your eye, but pursue only those that capture the heart."

– Indian Proverb

		LEFT	RIGHT
FAIRWAYS			
GREENS		LEFT	RIGHT
UP & DOWNS			
PUTTS			
18 HOLE SCORE			

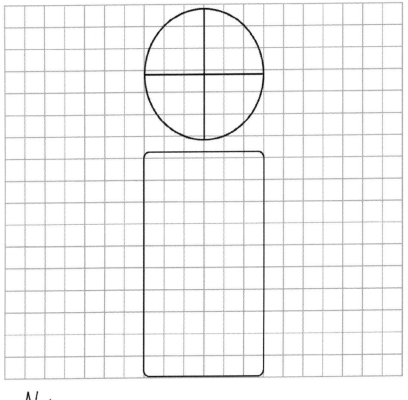

Notes

_____

_____

_____

_____

_____

_____

_____

Course: _____ **Date:** _____

"If you're offered a seat on a rocket ship, don't ask what seat!"

– Sheryl Sandberg

		LEFT	RIGHT
FAIRWAYS		LEFT	RIGHT
GREENS		LEFT	RIGHT
UP & DOWNS			
PUTTS			
18 HOLE SCORE			

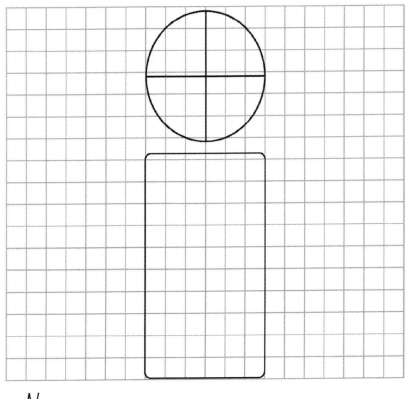

Notes

_____

_____

_____

_____

_____

_____

_____

_____

Close to winning a tournament?

Course: _____   Date: _____

"When one door of happiness closes, another opens, but often we look so long at the closed door that we do not see the one that has been opened for us. "

— Hellen Keller

FAIRWAYS		LEFT	RIGHT
GREENS		LEFT	RIGHT
UP & DOWNS			
PUTTS			
18 HOLE SCORE			

Why have you not sealed the deal? Next time, play to win. You have got this.

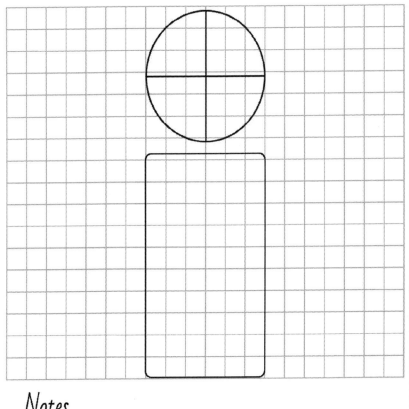

Notes

_____

_____

_____

_____

_____

_____

_____

_____

Course: _____   Date: _____

"Everything has beauty, but not everyone can see."

– Confucius

FAIRWAYS		LEFT	RIGHT
GREENS		LEFT	RIGHT
UP & DOWNS			
PUTTS			
18 HOLE SCORE			

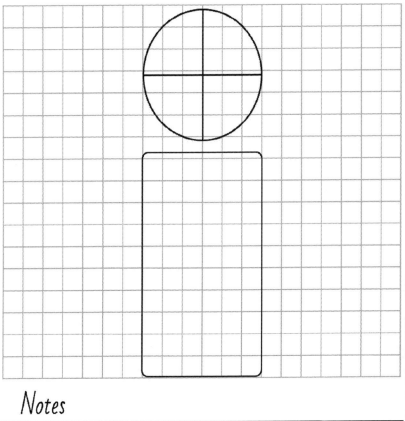

Notes

_____

_____

_____

_____

_____

_____

_____

Course: _____   Date: _____

"How wonderful it is that nobody need wait a single moment before starting to improve the world."

— Anne Frank

		LEFT	RIGHT
FAIRWAYS		LEFT	RIGHT
GREENS		LEFT	RIGHT
UP & DOWNS			
PUTTS			
18 HOLE SCORE			

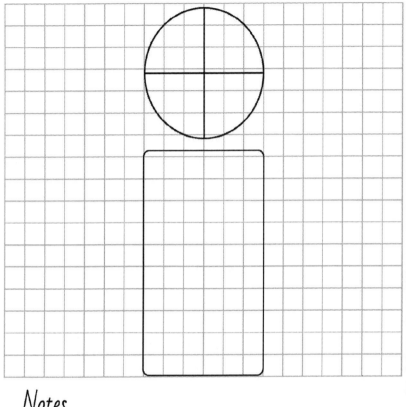

Notes

Course: Date:

"The only person you are destined to become is the person you decide to be."

– Ralph Waldo Emerson

		LEFT	RIGHT
FAIRWAYS		LEFT	RIGHT
GREENS			
UP & DOWNS			
PUTTS			
18 HOLE SCORE			

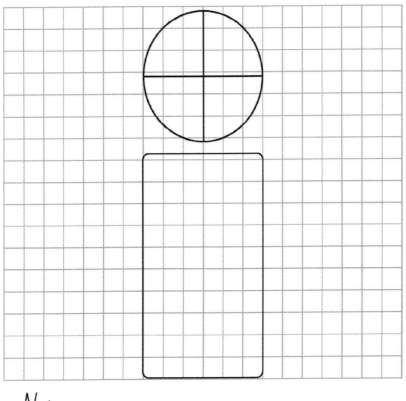

Notes

Course: _____   Date: _____

"Everything you've ever wanted is on the other side of fear."

– George Addair

FAIRWAYS		LEFT	RIGHT
GREENS		LEFT	RIGHT
UP & DOWNS			
PUTTS			
18 HOLE SCORE			

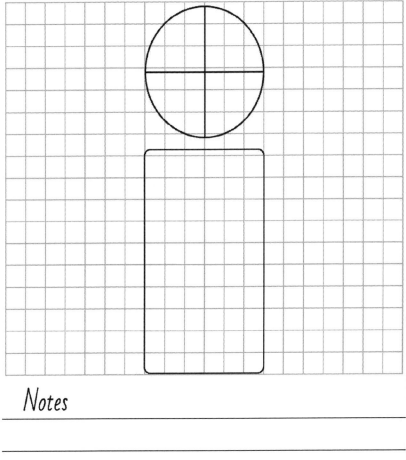

Notes

_____

_____

_____

_____

_____

_____

_____

_____

Course: _____ **Date:** _____

"We can easily forgive a child who is afraid of the dark; the real tragedy of life is when men are afraid of the light."

— Plato

		LEFT	RIGHT
FAIRWAYS			
GREENS		LEFT	RIGHT
UP & DOWNS			
PUTTS			
18 HOLE SCORE			

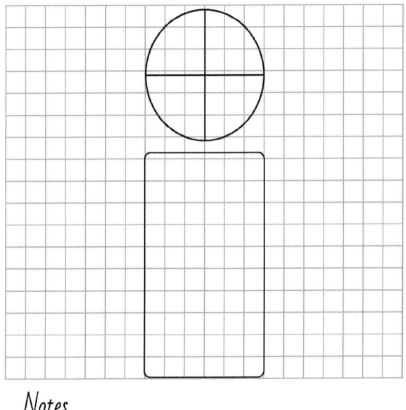

Notes

_____

_____

_____

_____

_____

_____

_____

_____

Course: Date:

"Nothing will work unless you do."

– Maya Angelou

		LEFT	RIGHT
FAIRWAYS		LEFT	RIGHT
GREENS		LEFT	RIGHT
UP & DOWNS			
PUTTS			
18 HOLE SCORE			

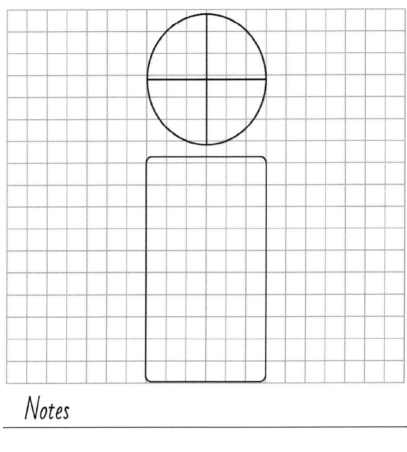

Notes

_____

_____

_____

_____

_____

_____

_____

PLAYER PERFORMANCE STATS

LUKE DONALD	SKILL	%	RANK
	Fairways	56.5	147th
	GIR (%)	61.92	176th
HEIGHT 5 ft, 9 in	Up & Downs	59.88	70th
WEIGHT 165 lbs	Puts Per Round	28.56	28th
BIRTHPLACE Hemel Hempstead, England	Driving Distance	278.5	178th
	Sand Saves	64.44	2nd
COLLEGE Northwestern University	Birdie Average	3.13	173rd
TURNED PRO 2001	Scoring Average	70.831	76th

JASON DAY	SKILL	%	RANK
	Fairways	53.94	172nd
	GIR (%)	63.72	139th
HEIGHT 6 ft, 0 in	Up & Downs	57.77	121st
WEIGHT 195 lbs	Puts Per Round	28.26	7th
BIRTHPLACE Beaudesert, Queensland, Australia	Driving Distance	306.2	19th
	Sand Saves	53.92	48th
COLLEGE	Birdie Average	4.15	6th
TURNED PRO 2006	Scoring Average	70.11	24th

How well do you plot your way around the course?

PLAYER PERFORMANCE STATS

TIGER WOODS (2000)	SKILL	%	RANK
	Fairways	71.22	54th
	GIR (%)	75.15	1st
HEIGHT	Up & Downs	67.08	3rd
6 ft, 1 in	Puts Per Round	28.76	36th
WEIGHT 185 lbs	Driving Distance	298	2nd
BIRTHPLACE Cypress, California	Sand Saves	57.27	51st
COLLEGE Stanford University	Birdie Average	4.92	1st
TURNED PRO 1996	Scoring Average	67.794	1st

TIGER WOODS (2008)	SKILL	%	RANK
	Fairways	60.71	139th
	GIR (%)	74.15	1st
HEIGHT	Up & Downs	62.81	10th
6 ft, 1 in	Puts Per Round	29.38	137th
WEIGHT 185 lbs	Driving Distance	306.4	6th
BIRTHPLACE Cypress, California	Sand Saves	55.17	29th
COLLEGE Stanford University	Birdie Average	4.65	1st
TURNED PRO 1996	Scoring Average	68.11	1st

In your next round, play for the fairways and leave the ego in car park.

IDEAS/NOTES/THOUGHTS

"Stay hungry. Stay foolish. Never let go of your appetite to go after new ideas, new experiences, and new adventures."

— Steve Jobs

MY YARDAGES

"Hit the shot you know you can hit, not the one you think you should."

– Dr Bob Rotella

Club	Full Shot	% Shot	% Shot

MY YARDAGES

"I never learned anything from a match that I won"

— Bobby Jones

Club	Full Shot	% Shot	% Shot

Your yardages can change over time, so here is another page for just that :)

No one is a self made man...

I am no expert, but merely a student sitting on the shoulders of giants.

If you find anything amazing in all three books, it is down to the lessons learned from those who have dedicated so much before me.

A special thanks to these golfing soldiers

- Peter Tarver Jones	- Laurie Canter	- Dave Alred
- Oscar Sharpe	- David Ray	- Brian Hemmings
- Phil Kenyon	- Mat Wallace	- David Galbraith
- Stuart Robinson	- Simon Cooper	- Tom King
- Gary Smith	- Eric Baldwin	- Andrew Serkitch
- Henry Manning	- Mark Bull	- Mat Perry
- John Gallen	- Peter Green	- Ian Marshall

Looking for more? Visit MakingAClubChampion.com

Actionable drills, tactics, and routines from the best in the game of golf. The specific advice and suggested purchases which you can test in your own game from tour players, phycologists, biomechanics instructors and much, much more. From their favorite books to personal action challenges. Each guest will inspire you to experiment and question everything. Start making your practice time more effective today.

What should you do next? Your free gift.

As a special thanks for purchasing your golfing journal. I have made another book, which I would like to send to you for free. How to structure your practice time can be difficult. With so many elements of the game to work on, we can get overwhelmed where to even start. From the lessons learned in the podcast. I have put together all of the notes, which resulted in:

"The Practice Principles - 5 Habits Every Golfer Should Stop Now."

If you would like these principles, all you have to do is
Email: makingaclubchampion@gmail.com or Visit:
www.makingaclubchampion.com/golf-journal
And you can start making your practice sessions more effective today.

CHRIS BAKER; broke par at age 13 and won his first, Men's Club Championship at age 15.

He went onto represent Great Britain and Ireland on the Swifts Tour competing in America. And was a winner on the Faldo Series.

Gaining a scholarship to America at University of Charlotte, North Carolina. He won two NCAA Conference Championships with his team.

He has won a combination of three Men's Club Championship's. And was part of the winning team at the Halford Hewitt in 2010, the biggest amateur tournament in the world.

The host of the show, 'Making A Club Champion.' Chris has always been interested in how the best coaches and players in the world of golf spend their time practicing and how to make that as effective as possible.

Chris has caddied multiple times on the European Tour at the dreaded final stage qualifying school.

He gained a strength and conditioning qualification in San Francisco and experiments in performance-based nutrition, competing in Ironman triathlons entirely on cashew butter, coconut oil, and medium chain triglycerides.

Chris is also an avid collector of Banksy artwork. He lives in Bristol, United Kingdom.

Made in the USA
Columbia, SC
07 August 2021

43178472R00065